WHAT IS SIN?

Written by Brittani Ramirez

Illustrations by Havilah G. Todd

WHY DO WE USE "YAH" & "YHWH"?

In our books, we call God "Yah" because it's a special way to say His Name. Did you know "God" is more like a title than His actual Name? It's like calling your dad "Dad" instead of using his real name!
In Hebrew, God's Name is written with four special letters:

YOD, HEY, VAV, HEY

In English, we write these letters as YHWH.
Some people pronounce His Name as "Yahuah," but a shorter, beautiful way to say it is "Yah." In fact, every time you say "HalleluYah," you're saying "Praise Yah!" How amazing is that?
We hope you enjoy this adventure, feel brave and loved, and remember that Yah is guiding you every step of the way!

Bobby was playing with his favorite
toy when he accidentally spilled juice
on the rug. When his mom asked
what happened, Bobby shrugged his
shoulders and said, "I don't know!"

His mom frowned
and said, "Bobby,
did you know telling
a lie is a sin?"

Bobby blinked.

"What is sin, mom?"

His mom replied, "It's anything that displeases God."

But Bobby was still confused.
"What displeases God?" He thought.
He decided to go on a mission to find out.

Bobby skipped next door to Miss Johnsons house. She went to church with them, surely she will know!

"Miss Johnson,
do you know
what sin is?"

Miss Johnson smiled and said , "Sin is different for everyone, Bobby. It's whatever the spirit tells you not to do."

Bobby scratched his head. But how can it be different for everyone? He wondered.

Later that day, Bobby went to the park and saw his friend Tommy. Bobby decided to ask him.
"Tommy, do you know what sin is?"

Tommy thought for a second,

"Well, my dad said it's like being sick, it's different for some people. For some it might be eating too much candy and for another it might be watching too much T.V".

Bobby confused once again thought about it. But what if I don't like candy or TV? How do I know what my sin is?

The next day Bobby went to church and decided to ask his youth pastor, "What is sin?"

She smiled and said, "Sin is breaking God's commandments. That's why we follow the Ten Commandments." Bobby tilted his head. "Then why don't we keep the rules of the Sabbath, like resting and setting it apart?"

The youth pastor hesitated. "We don't follow those rules anymore."

Bobby frowned. But didn't God tell Moses to keep all His commandments forever? he wondered.

After church, Bobby decided to ask the pastor.
Surely, he'd get a clear answer.

"What is sin?"

Bobby asked.
The pastor smiled warmly. "Sin, Bobby, is anything that separates us from God. It can be different for everyone—like being selfish, not praying, or even skipping church."

Bobby tilted his head, still confused. But how do I know for sure what separates me from God? he wondered.

Bobby felt defeated. Am I ever going to figure this out?
He thought to himself. Bobby went to his grandparents house for
dinner and decided to ask Grandpa.

"Grandpa, do you know what sin is?"

He chuckled and said
"Sin, Bobby,
is doing anything you wouldn't want
Jesus to see you do."

Bobby's eyes widened. Does that
mean even when I'm changing my
clothes, it's sin?

Bobby was tired and just about gave up.
Just then uncle Frank walked in the house for dinner.

Bobby, in a last effort, decided to ask Uncle Frank.

"Uncle Frank, I've been asking everyone,

'What is sin?'

and no one seems to have the same answer!" Bobby said.

Uncle Frank smiled and sat down beside Bobby.

"That's because, Bobby, not everyone goes straight to YHWH's Word for the answer. People have different ideas, but Yah has already given us the answer."

Bobby's eyes got wide. "He has? Where?"

Uncle Frank pointed to Bobby's Bible on the table. "Right here, Bobby. Always go to YHWH's Word. We can't always trust what people say, but we can always trust what YHWH says in the Bible.

"When someone tells you something,
you should test it by comparing it to the Bible."

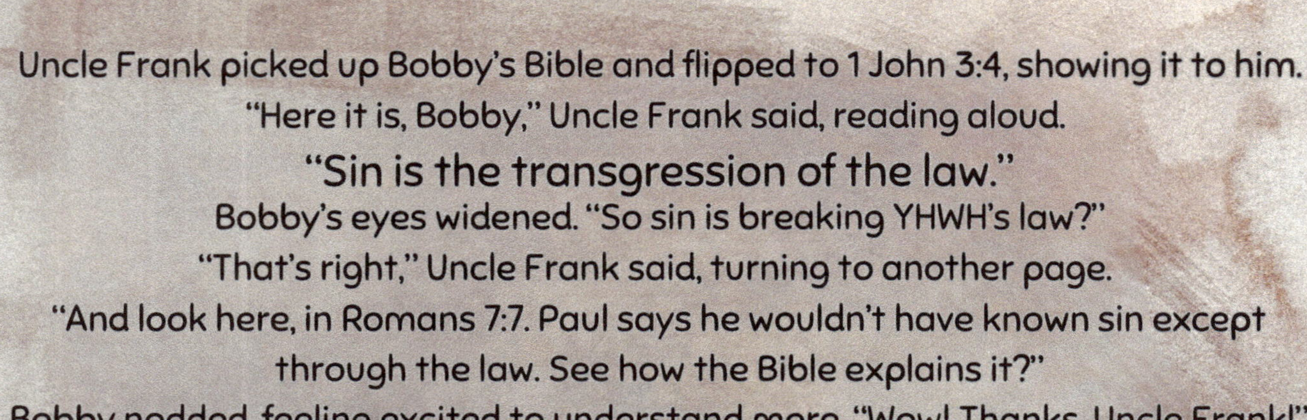

Uncle Frank picked up Bobby's Bible and flipped to 1 John 3:4, showing it to him.

"Here it is, Bobby," Uncle Frank said, reading aloud.

"Sin is the transgression of the law."

Bobby's eyes widened. "So sin is breaking YHWH's law?"

"That's right," Uncle Frank said, turning to another page.

"And look here, in Romans 7:7. Paul says he wouldn't have known sin except through the law. See how the Bible explains it?"

Bobby nodded, feeling excited to understand more. "Wow! Thanks, Uncle Frank!"

Bobby rushed to his mom. "Mom! I found out what sin is! It's when we break Yah's law!" His mom paused and looked at him curiously.

"Really? I didn't know that," she said thoughtfully. "How did you learn about it?"

Bobby grinned. "I read it in the Bible! And do you know why the Messiah came?"

His mom shook her head. "No, tell me," she said, intrigued.
Bobby beamed. "The Messiah came to forgive us when we sin and help us try again!"

His mom's face lit up. "That's amazing, Bobby. I think I need to read the Bible more to learn about these things too."
"Yeah!" Bobby said excitedly. "We can learn together!"

Bobby hugged Uncle Frank goodbye.
"Thanks for teaching me so much, Uncle Frank."

"Remember, Bobby, always test what others say with Yah's Word.
Acts 17:11 reminds us to check everything against the Scriptures."
Bobby nodded. "I will! Thanks, Uncle Frank!"
As he walked away, Bobby felt excited to read the Bible and learn even more.

That night, Bobby prayed,

"Thank you, Yah, for helping me learn what sin is. I'll try to do what's right and I'll go straight to your word to learn more, and I'm thankful that Yeshua will help me when I need it.
Amen."

BOBBY'S IMPORTANT LESSON!

Bobby learned such an important lesson!

We need to study YHWH's Word so we can know if what others tell us is true. Acts 17:11 talks about people who were wise because they checked everything against the Scriptures!

Messiah said in Matthew 22:37–40 that all of YHWH's laws and teachings hang on the first two commandments: to love YHWH with all your heart and to love your neighbor as yourself.

When we love something with all our heart,
it's a big deal

–it comes before everything else! That's why, when we love YHWH, we want to get to know Him by studying His Word. We also follow His ways, like keeping His Sabbath, which He says is a special sign between Him and His people forever
(Exodus 31:16–17).

And when we love our neighbor, we won't lie, cheat, steal, or hurt them. These things break YHWH's laws, but loving others helps us do what is right!

REFLECT ON BOBBYS JOURNEY

Bobby learned so much about YHWH's Word and how to follow His commandments. Now it's your turn to think about what you've learned! Take a moment to answer these questions and see how you can grow closer to YHWH, just like Bobby did.

- What is sin?

- Did you learn anything new from Bobby's journey?

- Why do you think YHWH gave us His commandments?

- How can you show love to YHWH with all your heart?

- What makes the Sabbath a special day, and how can you honor it?

- How can studying the Bible help you know YHWH better?

- What's one way you can show love to your neighbor today?

- Why is it important to test what others say with Scripture?

- What do you think it means to love YHWH more than anything else?

- If you make a mistake, what can you do to make it right?

SUPPORTING SCRIPTURES

1 John 3:4:
"Sin is the transgression of the law."

Romans 7:7:
"I wouldn't know what sin is without the law."

Exodus 20:1–17
The Ten Commandments.

Matthew 5:17:
"The Messiah said He came not to destroy the law, but to fulfill it."

James 1:22:
"Be doers of the Word, and not hearers only."

Romans 3:20:
"For by the law is the knowledge of sin."

SUPPORTING SCRIPTURES

Jeremiah 31:33:
"This is the covenant I will make with the people of Israel after that time," declares Yah.
"I will put my law in their minds and write it on their hearts. I will be their God, and they will be my people."

Hebrews 10:16:
"This is the covenant I will make with them after that time," says YHWH."
"I will put my laws in their hearts, and I will write them on their minds."

1 John 5:3:
"For this is the love of God, that we keep His commandments. And His commandments are not burdensome."

Revelation 14:12:
"Here is the patience of the saints; here are those who keep the commandments of Yah and the faith of Yeshua."

KEY PLACES TO FIND YHWH'S LAW

THE TEN COMMANDMENTS:
Exodus 20:1–17
Deuteronomy 5:6–21

DIETARY LAWS:
Leviticus 11

FEASTS & HOLY DAYS:
Leviticus 23

LOVING YHWH & HIS COMMANDS:
Deuteronomy 6:4–9
Psalm 119

LOVING YHWH & HIS COMMANDS:
Deuteronomy 6:4–9
Psalm 119

BLESSINGS & OBEDIENCE:
Deuteronomy 28

KEY PLACES TO FIND YHWH'S LAW

LAW WRITTEN ON OUT HEARTS:
Jeremiah 31:33
Hebrews 8:10
Ezekiel 36:26–27

THE MESSIAH & THE LAW:
Matthew 5:17–19
Romans 7:7
James 2:8–12

DEFINING SIN:
Romans 3:23
Romans 5:12
Romans 6:23
Romans 14:23
James 4:17
Proverbs 28:13
Isaiah 59:2
1 Corinthians 6:9–10
1 John 5:17

Looking for more books like this?

Looking for more books like this? Visit our website at www.scribblesandscriptures.com to explore more!

Love Our Books? Join Scribbles Book Club!

If you want all our books but don't want to buy them all at once, Scribbles Book Club is perfect for you! Get a new book delivered straight to your door every month, along with fun extras like stickers and bookmarks. Scan the QR code to start your monthly adventure today!